MEDIEVAL SILVER NEFS

VICTORIA AND ALBERT MUSEUM

Medieval Silver Nefs

by Charles Oman

LONDON
HER MAJESTY'S STATIONERY OFFICE
1963

Foreword

IN 1959 the museum was able to acquire the Burghley Nef, thanks to the generosity of the Worshipful Company of Goldsmiths and the National Art-Collections Fund. When it came to cataloguing it Mr Charles Oman, Keeper of the Department of Metalwork, discovered that nothing serious had been written for a very long time about *nefs* (the French name is used because they were hardly used in England), and that it was possible to throw fresh light upon the histories of several of the nine surviving examples. It was clearly opportune that a fresh approach should be made to this fascinating subject.

TRENCHARD COX

Introduction

IT is not surprising that medieval goldsmiths should have seized upon ship forms as a source of inspiration. The most widespread use of the motif was, of course, the incense-boat but in that case repeated copying usually resulted in the loss of resemblance to any sort of ship. This did not happen invariably, however, and the fine lines of the late fourteenth-century incense-boat once the property of Ramsey Abbey (FIG. 1) recall those of the early medieval ships with a figure-head at both ends (in this instance the ram's head used as the rebus of the abbey). The late fifteenth-century incense-boat belonging to the Chapel of the Constable of Castile in Burgos Cathedral (FIG. 2) has quite a realistic rendering of the planking of the hull and is complete with ports for the anchor-cable and a dragon figure-head, all closely copied from contemporary ships, only the towers upon the fo'c'sle and poop are completely fantastic. It would not be difficult to quote sixteenth-century incense-boats consciously imitating ship forms (some ape Roman galleys), but generally speaking there is little connection between the development of the incense-boat and that of the secular *nef*.[1]

Incense-boats need not detain us longer but something must be said about votive ships and ship reliquaries.

In days when it was customary to vow an appropriate thank-offering to some favoured church in memory of a special deliverance, it was inevitable that some should take the form of the vessel in which the devotee had escaped drowning. A number of foreign churches are still adorned with votive ships some of which date from the fourteenth century. The ordinary votive ship was of wood and only the aristocrats of the species were made in silver.[2] The most celebrated votive ship is the one which was vowed by Queen Marguerite of Provence to the church of Saint Nicolas de Port, near Varangéville, in Lorraine, in gratitude for the deliverance of herself, her husband St Louis and their three children, when caught in a storm whilst returning from Palestine in 1254. At the height of the storm she vowed a ship to the value of five marks of silver, taking the Sieur de Joinville to witness. On their safe return he tells us that:

'When the Queen (whom God absolve!) had returned to France she had the silver ship made at Paris. And there were in the ship the King, the Queen and the three children, all of silver; the sailors, the mast, the tillers and the ropes, all of silver; and the sails all sewn with silver wire. And the Queen told me that the making had cost a hundred *livres*.'[3]

It seems unlikely that *ex-voto* ships often reproduced so accurately the incident which they commemorated. For instance in 1508 Robert Barton, brother of the Scottish sea-captain Robert Barton, was paid £31 1s. 6d. for 'ane schip of silvir weyand xxxi ½ unce,

FIG. 1 The Ramsey Abbey Incense-boat. Silver parcel-gilt. English; last quarter of fourteenth century.
Victoria and Albert Museum

quhilk he offerit for the King in Sanct James in Spane' and since the French exchange rate is given, it is clear that the object was bought in France on the way to Compostella.[4] Though now rare, *nefs* were once ordinary articles of commerce and might be found in well-stocked goldsmiths' shops such as is depicted in the illuminated manuscript here illustrated[5] (FIG. 4).

The *ex-voto* ship was probably more often than not of secular origin. None of the *nefs* surviving in churches have anything distinctively religious about them. In medieval times pieces of secular plate were frequently given to popular shrines and no greater significance should be attached to the *nefs* than to drinking vessels, hunting-horns etc. still found in church treasuries. These have often been saved from appearing utterly incongruous by being adapted for some church use. In the case of *nefs* this meant conversion either into an incense-boat or into a reliquary. In the process the *nef* might lose much of its original character. Thus the secular origin of the *nef* of Anne of Brittany (PL. XII) which she converted into a reliquary of St Ursula, was not guessed until it was made evident by documents. In this case the conversion took place within a short time of its manufacture. Since a reliquary in the form of a ship would have been only appropriate for quite a limited number of saints, it is likely that few if any were made.[6]

Just as the ship form was used for more than one sort of religious vessel, so likewise secular *nefs* did not all serve the same purpose. Their uses and the usages connected with them, changed with the times. The earliest use would seem to have been as drinking

2

vessels and references in early French romances prove that they must have been in fairly general use as far back as the thirteenth century.[7] It is difficult to say how long *nefs* continued to be used as drinking vessels since the fairly full descriptions to be found in fourteenth-century inventories seldom allude to the use for which the pieces were intended. That *nefs* were still being used as drinking vessels in the second half of the fourteenth century is proved by a mention of 'a cup decorated with waves made in the form of a silver ship, gilt inside' amongst a list of the treasures of Pope Gregory XI in 1371.[8] It seems likely that the use of *nefs* for drinking was eventually abandoned because they were found to be hopelessly unsuited for that purpose.

Of the nine *nefs* ranging in date from the late fourteenth to the second quarter of the sixteenth century, which are the subject of this study, only the Zaragoza example (PL. III) and the Burghley Nef (PL. VIII) could now serve a practical purpose—both contain a salt-cellar in the poop. Some of the others have been gutted when being converted into reliquaries etc. but at least three can never have been more than ornaments.

The ornamental *nef* was what is now described as a status symbol. It was used to mark the place of the host at the dinner table, being placed not immediately in front of him but slightly to his left as may be seen in the illustration of a nobleman at dinner in the *Breviario Grimani* (FIG. 5). Occasionally a great *nef* was accompanied by a lesser one which served

FIG. 2 Incense-boat belonging to the Chapel of the Constable of Castile. Spanish; late fifteenth century.
Burgos Cathedral

3

FIG. 3 Votive *nefs* in the Church of St. Antonio di Castello, Venice. Detail from a painting (1515?) by Vettore Carpaccio. *Accademia di Belle Arti, Venice*

as a salt-cellar. Thus in the inventory of the plate owned by Charles V of France at the time of his death on 16 September 1380, are mentioned:

'Item, la grant nef du Roy, que la ville de Paris luy donna, toute plaine; pesant VI xx V marcs d'or.

'Item, la grant salière d'or, en façon d'une nef, que la ville de Paris donna au Roy, et est pareille a la grant nef dont cy-dessus est faicte mencion; pesant quinze marcs six onces d'or.'[9]

Another of the *nefs* belonging to the same king, is described as being made to contain his table utensils—a cup of essay, spoon, knife and fork.[10] A similar *nef* is mentioned in the account of the coronation banquet at Rheims of Charles VIII on 30 May 1484,[11] but there is little evidence that this variety was fashionable in medieval times. Later on the right to

FIG. 4 Interior of a goldsmith's shop *c.* 1460. Note the *nef* on the top shelf behind the counter. From an unidentified Flemish manuscript

FIG. 5 A nobleman at dinner. Note the *nef* a little to the right of his left hand. From the *Breviario Grimani*, Biblioteca S. Marco, Venice

use a *nef* containing table necessaries became in France a much sought after privilege but by this date the term had become a misnomer since the piece had lost all resemblance to a ship.[12] There is some slight evidence that the use of the ornamental *nef* for marking the place of the host, was already getting involved with questions of precedence even in medieval times. Illustrations of banquets seldom show more than the host's *nef*, but in a manuscript of the *Grands Chroniques de France* written between 1373–79 is an illustration[13] (FIG. 6) of the dinner given by Charles V of France to the Emperor Charles IV and his son Wenzel, King of Bohemia, in which a *nef* is shown before each of the monarchs. Too much should not be made of this, however, as in the representation of the same incident in the manuscript of the chronicle illustrated by Jean Foucquet in about 1460, no *nefs* are shown.[14]

It is clear that the use of *nefs* was widespread in France, Germany, Italy, the Low Countries and Spain in the later Middle Ages. Continental usages with regard to them did not catch on in England where they are only occasionally mentioned in fourteenth-century lists of the Royal Plate. The only visual representation of an English *nef* is in the British Museum copy of Walter de Milemete's treatise on the *Secreta Secretorum* of Aristotle, which is datable to the years 1326–27. It is four-legged and certainly not a drinking vessel since it is matched by an unmistakable covered cup (FIG. 8).[15]

The reason why the *nef* never came into general use in England was because its function of marking the place of the host at the dinner table was performed by the great salt. *Nefs* were not entirely unknown in this country in the latter part of the Middle Ages since there was one local variety. It is not clear how the alms *nef* was used but in 1404 William of Wykeham, Bishop of Winchester, bequeathed to Thomas Arundel, Archbishop of Canterbury, his newly fashioned silver alms dish in the form of a ship.[16] Otherwise mentions of *nefs* for alms appear to relate exclusively to royal pieces. One of silver-gilt with enamel was in the possession of Queen Philippa of Hainault, in 1348,[17] and there were two handsome examples amongst the plate taken over by Henry IV from Richard II in 1399.[18] These were far excelled by two which belonged to Henry VI in 1437.[19] One of these is described as being of silver-gilt and was filled with armed men fighting round the sides. The other was of gold and is described as follows:

'A grete ship called the Tygre garnysed with xix baleys (rubies), xii grete pearles and xiiij other smale pearles, the which weythe xxxiij mark. iij unces troy.'

Both of these had disappeared before the earliest Tudor inventory of the Royal Plate was compiled in 1521, nor does a *nef* of any type appear in any of the other sixteenth-century lists.

Though it was decided to confine this study to medieval examples, it must not be supposed that the manufacture of *nefs* ceased with the Renaissance. In France they became too closely associated with rigid rules of precedence and eventually the name survived any real

FIG. 6 King Charles V of France entertaining the Emperor Charles IV and his son Wenzel, King of Bohemia. Note the *nef* for each Sovereign. From MS. Fr. 2813. f.473v. in the Bibliothèque Nationale, Paris

FIG. 7 A typical *nef* of the decadence. Silver, parcel-gilt. Made by Esaias zur Linden of Nuremberg, *c.* 1620.
Victoria and Albert Museum. M.425–1956

FIG. 8 The only English representation of a *nef*. From British Museum, Add. MS. 47680. f.60v

resemblance to a ship. In Italy and Spain they appear to have declined in popularity after the second quarter of the sixteenth century. Their manufacture seems to have ceased in the Low Countries at about the same time and it is curious to note that they never formed part of the repertoire of Dutch goldsmiths at the period when Holland was a leading naval power. The popularity of the *nef* was not affected by the decline elsewhere in Europe. The age of clockwork arrived and gilt metal *nefs* were made which could run down the dinner table and lower the tension at tedious banquets. The number of *nefs* produced by the goldsmiths of Augsburg and Nuremberg in the latter part of the sixteenth and the early part of the seventeenth century must have been immense. It is not proposed to deal with them here since their artistic importance is not comparable with that of the pieces with which we have been dealing. In order to appreciate this it is only necessary to look at the illustration (FIG. 8) of an example made by Esaias zur Linden of Nuremberg (worked 1609–32), one of the principal makers of *nefs*. It will be observed that it neither makes any serious attempt to resemble a ship nor has the goldsmith lavished upon it any exceptional care.[20]

Designs and Iconography

IT has already been pointed out that some *nefs* were made to order whilst others were made by a goldsmith for stock. In the latter case the goldsmith was entirely responsible both for the design and execution. It seems likely also when a *nef* was commissioned for a presentation the goldsmith was generally left to design it and stipulations were only made as to armorial escutcheons etc. and cost. The *nefs* commissioned for the customer's own use would seem likely to have given much more trouble. Thus in 1512 the *priori* of Perugia placed an order for a new *nef* which was to be executed according to a design by the painter Pietro Perugino, by the goldsmith Mariotto di Marco under the supervision of two other named goldsmiths.[21]

In the ordinary course the goldsmith would seem to have been left to interpret the idea of the *nef* as he chose so that his ship was just any ship and no question of iconography arises. There were exceptions to this and it is obvious that Henry VI's alms *nef* known as the *Tygre* must have resembled a ship of that name. *Nefs* might also represent not real but imaginary vessels.

If the Burghley Nef is carefully examined it will be found that on the deck immediately in front of the main mast, ordinarily almost invisible, is a little cast group consisting of a man and woman clasping hands over a chessboard (FIG. 9). This is clearly intended to represent Tristran and Iseult who are recorded to have played chess in order to relieve the tedium of the voyage from Ireland to Cornwall.[22] Clearly they are just beginning to feel the effects of the fatal love-potion. So far no other example nor mention of a *nef* depicting an incident from a romance has been noted. This does not mean that they were exceptionally rare since the tiny figures on the Burghley Nef are so inconspicuous that they might easily have escaped the eye of the maker of an inventory. There is a further reason for supposing that the subject had been used before. The little figures are dressed in the costume of the late fourteenth century, which suggests that they were cast from a model which had been lying about in the workshop for a very long time.

Some *nefs* of which we have record, were clearly intended to illustrate some theme which it is not at all easy always to recognise. Thus in the year 1395 Louis, Duke of Orleans, got his goldsmith Aubertin to service what must have been his principal *nef*[23] 'afin qu'elle feust mieulx et plus chièrement vendue'. The description is much too long for quotation but makes it clear that the piece was of the richest sort and was adorned with religious subjects which it is not easy to link together into a coherent theme. The ship was of gold set with precious stones but the base was silver-gilt. On the fo'c'sle and the poop, respectively, were figures of the Virgin and Gabriel (the Annunciation), round the deck were figures of the Twelve Apostles enamelled in divers colours. On the bridge were the Four

Evangelists decorated with enamel and another four left plain. Above rose a great cross in the likeness of a sail enamelled blue and *semée de fleurs de lis d'or.* and with a Crucifix surrounded by eight gold angels, enamelled white. Above the sail was the figure of the Almighty holding an orb and cross and richly enamelled. About the ship were a number of other personages including an emperor, a king in armour, an angel in armour, two further representations of God the Father and eight of 'Addam et de Eve, esmaillez de blanc, comme nuz'.

Of the nine surviving *nefs* three are supported by sirens (PL. VIII, XV and XVIII) but this does not suggest an allusion to any particular legend. Sirens who by the sweetness of their singing lured sailors to their doom, formed a generally recognised navigational risk

12

FIG. 10 Spoon. *Victoria and Albert Museum.* 1392–1888

in medieval times. So did dragons, though the winged one which supports the Zaragoza Nef (PL. III) is, perhaps, unusual in this context.

When a *nef* was not mounted on some sort of base it was equipped with wheels, as are two of the examples at Toledo (PL. IV and VI). This form of mounting was already widely used in the fourteenth century.[24]

13

Surviving Nefs

IT is not intended to provide in this section full catalogue descriptions but only to give the reader such information, both factual and historical, as has not been already supplied or which does not fit appropriately into the final discussion on ship models.

The earliest and largest of the surviving *nefs* (PL. I) is that which was bequeathed to Toledo Cathedral by Archbishop Pedro Tenorio (1377–99). It would appear to be Spanish work of the second half of the fourteenth century. The hull is much less romanticised than usual, the lower part being constructed in strips in imitation of timbers whilst a gilt band about the level of the deck is engraved on both sides in black letter with the well-known charm, IESUS AUTEM TRANSIENS PER MEDIUM ILLORUM IBAT.[25] Around the poop is another gilt band engraved with arcading of a distinctly Moorish character. The whole is supported on a spreading hexagonal foot engraved with conventional foliage. On alternate sides are applied small quatrefoil escutcheons, originally decorated with translucent enamel, bearing shields engraved with the donor's arms, a lion rampant. The hull is empty and there is nothing to indicate how it was filled originally. In place of the mast is an Ionic column surmounted by a little temple on the top of which is a seated figure of San Blas. Though this part can only date from the early years of the seventeenth century, it is known that the archbishop intended the *nef* to be used to contain relics.[26]

The *nef* (PL. III) presented to Zaragoza Cathedral by the Valencian corsair Juan de Torrellas, would appear to be Spanish work of the early part of the fifteenth century. In 1482 a thief stole the diamond which at that time adorned the forehead of the dragon and, according to Bertaux,[27] stole the base as well. The damage would appear to have been even more serious, as only the part above the water-line would appear to be original. In 1505 Maestre Lope, a goldsmith of Zaragoza, was given the fragments to repair. These would seem not to have included the original nautilus shell, since the present one is a bad fit so that the goldsmith had to supply a piece of silver chased with waves, to fill up part of the aperture of the shell. This piece is obviously of the same period as the foot. The dragon, which is decorated with green enamel, dates also probably from the 1505 restoration.

The second and third *nefs* in the treasury of Toledo Cathedral may be dated between 1425–75 and illustrate different varieties of the luxurious art of the goldsmiths of Venice. One of them is traditionally believed to have belonged to Dona Mencia Enriquez de Toledo (*d.* 1479),[28] second wife of Beltran de la Cueva, Duke of Albuquerque, and the other to Joanna the Mad, daughter of Ferdinand and Isabella and mother of the Emperor Charles V.[29]

Though Dona Mencia's *nef* (PL. IV) is now little more than a wreck, it must have been originally an attractive fantasy, though it makes so little attempt at realism that it will not be necessary to discuss it as a ship model. There is now no indication as to how it was fitted out internally and the winged dragon at the prow has lost both its head and tail. The lower part of the hull is made of crystal and is in fair condition but the upper part is of silver-gilt divided into oblong panels upon each of which is scratched a number. These panels were originally set with plaques decorated with foliage made up out of stamped leaves and wire—a technique which is found on a small group of pieces made at Venice in the second half of the fifteenth century. The character of the missing plaques can be recovered from a plaque surviving on the stern (PL. V). The wheels are original and are decorated similarly.

Time has not treated more kindly the *nef* of Joanna the Mad. The part of the hull which would be above the water-line and the framework which holds the crystal and serves as the keel, are all that remain of the original design. Since the framework shows considerable signs of alteration, it is clear that the original crystal hull has been lost. The mast contains a relic of Santa Leocadia mounted up in crystal and silver-gilt. The relics of this saint were brought back to Toledo on 26 April 1587, and probably the *nef* suffered a thorough overhaul (including a new set of wheels), when it was converted into a reliquary. The upper part of the hull is divided into three tiers of oblong panels decorated with stamped ornaments (crescents, stars, flowers and beading), set in dark blue and green enamel.[30] The framework with the keel are similarly decorated.

The *nef* is not identical with one[31] (probably an incense-boat) included amongst the chapel plate in a 1545 inventory of the possessions of Joanna but it may be the same as one of which there is a lengthy but difficult description amongst the plate of her parents 'The Catholic Kings' preserved in the Alcazar at Segovia in November 1503.[32]

The Burghley Nef was in a remarkably good state of preservation when it was purchased for the Museum in 1959. It was only necessary to supply fresh silver wire for the rigging and put back in their proper places some of the sails which had been misplaced at some time in the nineteenth century. The pennons at the mast heads had probably been provided at the same time.

The importance of the piece was first recognised when Mr Arthur Grimwade was engaged on making an inventory of the plate at Burghley House after the death of the 5th Marquess of Exeter in 1956. It was not until it had passed through Christie's that its full interest was realised—that the maker's mark (FIG. 11) was the *fleur-de-lis couronnée et au-dessous deux bannières en croix de St André* used by the Paris goldsmith Pierre le Flamand who is first mentioned in the year 1462.[33] The *nef* also bears the date-letter of a *crowned Y* which Christie's took to be that for 1505. This would mean that Pierre le Flamand had an unusually long working-life, and there appears to be no real objection to the attribution of this date-letter (otherwise unknown) to the previous cycle and the year 1482. Pierre le

FIG. 11 Mark of
Pierre le Flamand and Paris
year-letter for 1482–83.
The Burghley Nef

Flamand was apparently in full activity at this period and served as *garde* of the Paris goldsmiths in 1478, 1483 and 1489.

The iconography of the *nef* has already been discussed whilst its value as a ship model will be dealt with in the next section. It only remains to tell the little that is known about its history. The first reference to the *nef* in the Burghley House plate book is a note added to the 1824 inventory and dated 1844. At the end of the same inventory is added a list of plate including 'one small ship' received from Cowdray in 1842. This plate was part of the share of the then Marchioness of Exeter of the inheritance of the last Viscount

Montague. No inventories of the plate at Cowdray appear to have survived, so that there is no means of knowing how the *nef* found its way to Sussex.[34]

That the history of the *nef* in the treasury of Rheims Cathedral was not straightforward, was apparent to Alfred Darcel[35] in 1881, but it has been left to the present monograph to supply the missing link which proves that it was made for a secular use for Anne of Brittany during the period of her marriage to Louis XII.

It seems best to trace its history backwards from the time of its presentation by Henri III in 1574, which is attested by a lengthy inscription. It will be seen that in its present state the piece consists of a ship having a hull of jasper mounted fancifully with a trellised bulwark broken by seven turrets with conical roofs. On the deck are eleven figures representing St Ursula and her companions. All are enamelled but six are of gold and five (of inferior quality) are of silver. In the prow there is a diminutive figure in armour, perhaps a survivor from the original crew. The mast looks as if it had been formed from a palm tree and is surmounted by an angel (probably Fortune but she has lost her sail). The top is decorated with little oval shields bearing the well-known monogram of H with two crossed Cs used by Henri II and Catharine de' Medici. The ship rests on a coronet which stands in the middle of a hexagonal base enamelled green to represent waves. The sides of the base bear the donor's arms as King of France and of Poland, a scroll bearing the dedicatory inscription and another alluding to the relics of St Ursula and her companions.[36]

Darcel never doubted that the piece dated from 1574, attributing the H and crossed C monogram to Henri III and his mother, instead of recognising it as evidence that the piece was not all of one period. Though Marquet de Vasselot had already arrived at the conclusion that the *nef* dated from a much earlier period than 1574 it was left to Pierre Verlet[37] to elaborate this view. That the costumes worn by St Ursula and her companions were such as were in use in the late fifteenth and early sixteenth century was obvious but more interesting was the discovery of a goldsmith's mark underneath the base (FIG. 12).

FIG. 12 Mark of Pierre Rousseau of Tours. *Nef of Anne of Brittany*

This consists of *a letter R below two towers surmounted by a crown*. This he recognised as the mark of a Tours goldsmith having a surname beginning with the letter R. Furthermore he discovered the record of the purchase of plate in 1516 by François I from Robin Rousseau, goldsmith of Tours. This suggestion would appear to be entirely convincing if it were not for a document[38] which seems to show that the *nef* was in existence eleven years earlier. On 3 June 1505, Jehan de Paris, painter and page of the king and queen, signed a receipt for a quantity of plate all of which had been made by Henry, the King's goldsmith, except the last item which is described as follows:

'Plus a receu une petite navire d'or & d'argent, garnye de plusieurs efscussons, aux armes du Roy & de la Royne, que la dicte dame a faict prendre pour mectre les unze mil vierges'

The conclusion appears to be inevitable that this is a description of the Rheims Nef in its original state, since it is most unlikely that there would have been two *nefs* fitted out as reliquaries of St Ursula and the Eleven Thousand Virgins. If this view be accepted, it would appear that whilst in secular use the sides of the ship were hung with shields, a common practice in medieval times. This would have much enhanced its appearance by covering up some of the rather clumsy trelliswork. The six enamelled gold figures must have been added in 1505 when the *nef* was turned over for conversion into a reliquary, the five silver-gilt figures must be replacements dating from one of the two subsequent restorations. The undersized figure of a knight is presumably a survivor from the original crew. A restoration in the time of Henri II included the provision of the mast adorned with the tell-tale escutcheons with the H and crossed C monogram. The second restoration was when the *nef* was furbished up for presentation to Rheims Cathedral and included the royal arms and the dedicatory inscription.

If the view be accepted that the piece is at least eleven years earlier than was suggested by Verlet, it follows that the maker's mark is not that of Robin Rousseau whose name is only found in the Tours accounts from 1511 onwards, but that of his father Pierre who can be traced back to 1474.[39]

The technical description of the Schlüsselfelder Nef will be deferred until the following section. It is not known how or when it came into the possession of the family whose name it bears and who still own it. It is in a remarkably good state of preservation and the original design has never been modified. It bears the Nuremberg mark[40] but no maker's mark since the use of these was not yet obligatory. The case bears the date 1503. If this be taken as approximately the date of manufacture, it becomes difficult to attribute it to the most renowned Nuremberg goldsmith of the day, Albrecht Dürer the Elder who died in 1502 aged seventy-five years. On the other hand Hans Krug the Elder (master in 1484; died in 1516) would seem to have stood high in the esteem of his contemporaries but no surviving piece of plate has been attributed to him.

The *nef* in the treasury of the Basilica di S. Antonio at Padua, will be discussed in its technical aspects in the following section. It is also in a remarkably good state of preservation. Nothing much appears to have been lost and the only accretions are two little trees which have been planted incongruously one over the hold and the other on the poop. There is no mark but the piece is clearly akin to the Schlüsselfelder Nef. If a date about 1500 be accepted for the latter, it would seem fair to date the *nef* at Padua some fifteen years later. Although the general effect is still Gothic, there is a distinct intimation of the advent of the Renaissance in the treatment of the siren. This intermingling of styles is very characteristic of the work of Ludwig Krug (*d.* 1532), second son of Hans Krug who has already been mentioned.[41]

Whereas the Schlüsselfelder Nef has received scant attention from writers, the present one has attracted a certain amount of conjecture, all of which has been misdirected. Father Gonzati, seizing upon the one unoriginal feature, suggested that the little trees proved a connection with the Della Rovere family and Pope Sixtus IV (*d.* 1484), although he admitted that the first documentary reference to the piece was in an inventory of 1537.[42] More recently W. Arslan claimed it as the work of a Ferrarese goldsmith of the fifteenth century working under the influence of Cosmè Tura.[43] Although it is certainly true that the Este family liked *nefs*, it does not seem possible to identify the present one with any of those mentioned in the inventories which have been published.[44]

The *nef* which reached the British Museum with the Franks Bequest, is the latest of those which can fairly be described as medieval. Although the treatment of the ship is still Gothic, the stem and base are in the early Renaissance style. This mixture of styles was current over most of western Europe in about 1530. The triangular knop is inscribed PLVS PENSEER QVE DIER. All that is known about it is that it was formerly the property of the Swiss family of the Barons d'Alt de Tieffenthal and probably mainly because of this, it has been described as Swiss, Sir Hercules Read and A. B. Tonnochy commenting 'It has peculiarities that may well be considered French, but on the whole its production at Syon or at some other centre in the Rhône valley seems more likely'.[45] It seems hardly likely that so sophisticated a piece could have been made in the little town on which they picked, though this objection would not apply to some of the larger Swiss towns. On the other hand the sixteenth century was the golden age of the Swiss mercenary so that plate with merely a Swiss provenance may represent loot from almost anywhere.

Plus penser que dire has been used as the motto of the town of Bar-le-Duc from at least the first half of the seventeenth century and probably earlier. This seems to suggest the possibility that the *nef* may have originated somewhere in Lorraine.[46]

Nefs as Ship Models

WHILST the decorativeness of the ship motif was generally recognised, the goldsmith would appear seldom to have allowed himself to exploit it to the full, even if he so desired. If he decided that the hull should be made from a shell, mother-o'-pearl or crystal, the realism of the design would be bound to suffer. Moreover it would almost seem that the romance of the ship was felt most strongly in places remote from the sea. Had Pierre le Flamand who made the Burghley Nef, Pierre Rousseau who made the Rheims Nef, or the two South German goldsmiths who made the Schlüsselfelder and Padua Nefs ever seen a real ship? Had they sketched a ship when visiting some port or were they entirely dependant on drawings by other artists? It seems only too likely that the goldsmiths were forced to borrow their nautical knowledge, but whilst extreme caution must be used in using *nefs* as evidence as to the appearance of medieval ships, it would be wrong to discount them entirely. Caution must be used for the goldsmith may have used a drawing of an old-fashioned ship. Thus in a 1329 inventory of the English Royal Plate is listed 'a silver *nef* with four wheels and a gilt head of a dragon at either end of the said ship'.[47] We are left in doubt as to whether the design was out of date or the *nef* was a very old one. Ships with figure heads at each end were in general use when the Bayeux Tapestry was made but would appear to have been obsolete by the beginning of the thirteenth century.

Of the surviving *nefs* the one bequeathed by Archbishop Tenorio (1377–99) to Toledo Cathedral is undoubtedly the oldest. It will be seen that the form of the hull resembles closely those of the two ships in a drawing in a psalter once the property of the priory of St Bartholomew, Smithfield (FIG. 13). Though this drawing is usually dated about 1330, the *nef* was made in the last quarter of the century.

Next in date is the *nef* presented to Zaragoza Cathedral by the Valencian corsair Juan de Torrellas. In this case, for reasons which have already been explained, it is necessary to ignore everything which would be below the water-line. It will then be found that the upper portion gives quite a factual representation of a ship at a rather later date than the one which has just been considered. It is still single-masted but it will be noted that the fo'c'sle and poop have grown in importance. Right over the stern is a temporary pent-house such as was used in summer. This feature was destined to become more prominent later on. It will be observed that no guns are carried. A date early in the fifteenth century is suggested for it.

Though the *nef* of Joanna the Mad at Toledo Cathedral (PL. VI) must date from the latter part of the century, it appears to be a much romanticised version of the same sort of vessel. It is only necessary to draw attention to the fantastically large dragon figure-head and to the framework for the awnings over the fo'c'sle and the poop.

Of the remaining *nefs* four represent, with varying degrees of accuracy, the type of ship in use in the fifteenth and early years of the sixteenth century. The principal characteristics of these can be seen in a drawing of ships in a storm (FIG. 14) from the celebrated pictorial life of Richard Beauchamp, Earl of Warwick, in the British Museum, which is dated 1485–90 and in the engraving of the *Kraeck* by the Flemish artist W A of about the same date (FIG. 15). It will be noted that the ships are three-masted and have much more elaborate fo'c'sles and poops over which can be seen the timbers for supporting the awning for the temporary pent-house. The *Kraeck* has a dragon figure-head but carries no guns, the ships in the English drawing are exactly the opposite in these respects.

Though the Burghley Nef is the least realistic of the four *nefs* of this type, it is unique in being exactly dated by the Paris year-letter for 1482–83. The form of the hull has been dictated by that of the nautilus shell from which it is formed but the upper parts illustrate quite well recent developments in naval architecture. There are three masts, the main and fore masts both carrying main and topsails, the mizzen carries a lateen sail and the bowsprit a small square sail. The fo'c'sle and poop are both enclosed by battlemented arcading. The deck of the fo'c'sle is open, that of the poop is occupied by a saltcellar. The dragon figure-head has not been allowed to get out of all proportion, as has happened in some other examples. The ship is heavily gunned—too heavily, one of the guns on the poop is aimed directly at the foot of the mainmast!

The German goldsmiths responsible for the Schlüsselfelder Nef at Nuremberg (PL. XVI)

FIG. 14 Ships in the Channel. From British Museum, MS. Julius. E. IV. f.25

22

FIG. 15 A carrick (*kraeck*). *Ashmolean Museum, Oxford*

23

and the example in the Basilica di Sant' Antonio, Padua, allowed only a certain romanticism to dilute their realism. Though both represent a ship of essentially the same design, they differ considerably in character. The Schlüsselfelder Nef is well found but not over-gunned like the Burghley Nef. The artist has chosen to depict a ship at a moment when an alarm has just been given. Armed men are standing to whilst the seamen are busily un-furling the sails. Ammunition of some sort is being hauled up into the top so that it can be thrown down when the enemy closes. What do the bags contain? Are they filled with lime or merely with stones? It is probably a grappling iron, rather than an anchor, which dangles from the prow, since it is suspended by a chain instead of a cable. There is no sign of flurry about the *nef* at Padua, which appears to be about to sail in its own time. Standing on the bulwark of the fo'c'sle a sailor empties a bottle of drink whilst under the awning behind him stand a knight and his page. A sailor is seen running down a ladder from the fo'c'sle into the well of the ship where the holds are covered by hinged hatches. The poop is built-in, unlike that of the Nuremberg example which has only got the frame for a temporary awning. Over the stern are five windows, two of which are shuttered (PL. XXII). Through one is seen a man with a sword, a passenger leans out of another and appears to be talking to a page (or a dwarf?) whose head only appears above the next windowsill. The richly carved rail surrounding the fo'c'sle and poop suggest that this is a luxury ship—the sort of ship in which a rich noble would make the pilgrimage to the Holy Land. She carries no guns. For reasons which have been explained, it seems likely that both *nefs* should be dated within the first fifteen years of the sixteenth century.

The *nef* in the British Museum (PL. XXII) may also be classed as a romanticised but fairly realistic representation of a late medieval ship. It is in full sail but none of the crew is visible. Alone of the surviving *nefs* it retains its rudder. Both the fo'c'sle and poop are roofed over, the latter in two sections. At the sides protrude numerous guns which alternate with shields (a feature frequently encountered in contemporary drawings of ships). The upper part of the hull is very inappropriately decorated with stamped hunting-scenes. The lower part was probably either of crystal or shell but only a silver cage remains. It is a typical example of Northern art of about 1530 with its tendency towards over elaboration.

Whilst it has been possible to find some ressemblance between the seven *nefs* which we have just described, with real medieval ships, there remain two examples which make no attempt at all at realism. The *nef* of Dona Mencia Enriquez de Toledo in Toledo Cathedral (PL. IV) and that of Anne of Brittany in Rheims Cathedral (PL. XII) can be regarded only as fantasies.

Notes

1 It was the fate of some secular *nefs* to be bequeathed to churches where they were used as incense-boats. Since they were quite unsuited for this purpose it is not surprising that they did not affect designs.

2 Besides real silver ship models there would appear to have been some cheap lines in little representations of ships cast or stamped out of silver. A lot of these adorned the monument of the popularly canonised Archbishop Scrope in York Minster (*Fabric Rolls of York Minster*, Surtees Society, XXXV, 1859, 225–6).

3 'Quant la royne (que Diex absoille !) fu revenue en France, elle fist faire la nef d'argent à Paris. Et estoit en la nef, li roys, la royne, et li tri enfant, tuit d'argent; li mariniers, li mas, li gouvernaus et les cordes, tuit d'argent; et li voiles tous cousus a fil d'argent. Et me dist la royne que la façons avoit coustei cent livres.'
The ship appears to have been lost during the seventeenth century but the exact date is unknown (Émil Badel, *Le Voeu de St Louis à l'église de Saint Nicolas de Port*, 1918, pp. 24–27).

4 Sir James Balfour Paul, *Accounts of the Lord High Treasurer of Scotland*, IV, 1902, pp. 40–41.

5 H. Nocq when illustrating this picture in *Le Poinçon de Paris*, 1931, IV, said that it was taken from a manuscript in the Bibliothèque Nationale. This appears to be a mistake and I have failed to trace the source.

6 There is a unique reference of 1380 to a ship monstrance: 'Ung reliquaire d'or en façon d'une nef, à porter le corps Nostre Seigneur, que deux angelotz soustiennent; et poise neuf marcs, sept onces d'or.' J. Labarte, *Inventaire du mobilier de Charles V, roi de France*, 1879, p. 46.

7 Thus:
> *Une grant nef tote d'or fin*
> *Qui estoit plainne de bon vin*

(Raoul de Houdenc, *La Vengence Raguidel*, ed. Mathias Friedwagner, Halle, 1909, p. 23, vv. 735–6) or
> *Devant Gerbert porte Fromons la nef;*
> *Tote fu plainne de vin et de claré.*

(*Gerbert de Metz*, ed. Pauline Taylor, Namur-Louvain-Lille, 1953, vv. 12993–4).

8   *Item 1 ciphus undatus factus ad modum navete argenti deauratus ab intra* (Hermann Hoberg, *Die Inventare des päpstlicher Schatzes in Avignon, 1314–76*, Rome, 1944, p. 411).

9   J. Labarte, *op cit.*, pp. 64 and 77.

10   *Item, la navecte goderonné, et mect-on dedans, quant le Roy est a table, son assay, sa cueiller, son coutelet et sa fourchette* (*Ibid.* p. 109).

11   *Et devant luy sur la table du costé dextre y en avoit une plus grande [couronne?] sur un coussin de drap d'or, et sur ladite table a senestre, y avoit une grande nef d'argent doré en laquelle estoit le e linge de bouche pour sa personne* (D. Godefroy, *Le Ceremonial François*, 1649, I, p. 206).

12   See H. Havard, *Dictionnaire de l'Ameublement*, I, cols. 502–6 under *Cadenas* and III, cols. 978–82 under *Nef*. For the history of the *Caddinet* in England see *Burlington Magazine*, C, 1958, pp. 431–5.

13   Paris, Bibliothèque Nationale MS. Fr. 2813, f. 473 v. Part of the entertainment was a masque showing the exploits of Godefroid de Bouillon. This is seen in the lower part of the picture.

14   Paris, Bibliothèque Nationale, MS. Fr. 6465, f. 446 v.

15   British Museum Add. MS. 47680, f. 60 v., formerly at Holkham. There is no similar picture in the contemporary manuscript in the library of Christ Church, Oxford.

16   R. Lowth, *Life of William of Wykeham*, 1759, app. xxxviii. Continental references to *nefs* in connection with alms are rather earlier in date but equally obscure e.g.— 'Item a le aumosne, une nef et 1 pot d'argent' mentioned amongst the treasure of the Count of Hainault in 1304 (Dehaisnes, *Documents . . . concernant l'histoire de l'art en la Flandre, l'Artois et le Hainault*, 1886, I, p. 154).

17   *Archaeologia*, XXXI, 1846, 79 and 379.

18   F. Palgrave, *Antient Kalendars and Inventories of the Exchequer*, 1836, III, pp. 324–5.

19   For the first *nef* Palgrave, *op. cit.*, II, p. 165. The *Tygre* is variously described in the same vol. pp. 144, 166, 171 and 243.

20 For collections of illustrations of later *nefs* see *Pall Mall Magazine*, X, 1896, pp. 517–25; *The Connoisseur*, CXI, 1943, pp. 90–95; *Argentor*, V, 1950, 213–22 and Friederich Moll, *Das Schiff in Bildenden Kunst*, Bonn, 1929, pl. I.

21 In view of this excessive supervision, it is not surprising that this *nef* was not completed until 1535. It was very elaborate and apart from the crew carried figures of San Ercolano (a former bishop of Perugia), a crowd of *bambini*, two horses with bells round their necks, and a figure of Fortune—presumably at the mast-head (Angelo Angelucci, *Della Oreficeria Perugina dal XIII alla prima meta del XVI secolo*, Perugia, 1853, pp. 17 and 23.

22 'Au quart jour se jouoit Tristan aux eschès a Yseuelt, et faisoit si grant chault que trop. Tristan oult soif, si demanda du vin etc.' *Le Roman de Tristan par Thomas*, ed. Joseph Bedier, Paris, 1905, II, p. 341.
   Long before the discovery of the Burghley Nef Professor R. S. Loomis had noted the use of the Tristran legend in the decoration of plate (*Arthurian legends in medieval art*, 1938, pp. 28–29).

23 A. Champollion—Figeac, *Louis et Charles, Ducs d'Orleans, leur influence sur les arts, la litterature, et l'esprit de leur siècle*, Paris, 1844, II, 21–23.

24 Of nine *nefs* listed in the Papal Treasury at Avignon in 1360, three had wheels (Hoberg, *op. cit.*, p. 381). This would appear to have been about the normal proportion.

25 This quotation from *Luke* IV, 30, seems to have been used particularly as a charm against sudden danger, particularly against attack by robbers. Thus Sir John Mandeville says (*Travels*, ch. X) 'therefore seyen some men when thei dreden them of thefes on any way, or of enemys, *Jesus autem etc.*' It was popularly believed by contemporaries that when Edward III used this inscription together with a representation of a ship on the *noble* issued in 1344, it was an allusion to his escape from danger when he passed through the French fleet at the battle of Sluys four years earlier (*Chronicon Monasterii de Melsa*, Rolls Series, III, 45).

26 In his will the archbishop bequeathed 'la nuestra nave de plata que fezimos en Sevilla' to Santa Maria la Blanca which had been a church in early times but which had latterly been used as a synagogue. The project of reconverting the building into a church was evidently already planned but was only effected by St Vincent Ferrer six years after the death of Archbishop Tenorio. The *nef* would seem to have fallen to

the residuary legatee, the chapel of San Blas which had been built and endowed by the archbishop and where he lies buried. He left the following directions 'we wish that there be made a mast of silver with its rigging, and at the top of the mast its topsail with our arms, and that some relics be put in it, so that this *nef* may be carried in processions and may be placed on the altars at the principal festivals'. Eugenio Narbona, *Historia de D. Pedro Tenorio, Arcobispo de Toledo*, Toledo, 1624, p. 122.

27 Real Junta del Centenario de los Sitios de 1808–9, Zaragoza, *Exposiçion Retrospectiva de Arte*, 1908, p. 225.

28 She was the oldest daughter of Don Garcia Alvarez de Toledo, Duke of Alba de Tormes and of Doña Maria Enriquez de Toledo, daughter of Don Fadrique Enriquez, Grand Admiral of Castile and Leon. She married Don Beltran on 13 June 1476 (F. F. de Béthencourt, *Historia Genealogica y Heraldica de la Monarquia Española*, X, 1920, pp. 233-5).

29 An unfortunate confusion has arisen with regard to the attributions of these two *nefs*. Ramon Perro, *Toledo en la mano*, Toledo, 1857, I, pp. 453 and 609, makes it quite clear that it was the *nef* containing the relic of Santa Leocadia which was given by Joanna the Mad. This has been followed by the latest published account of the cathedral by Canon J. F. Rivera (*La Cathédrale de Toléde*, 1957, p. 38). On the other hand it was the *nef* at present under discussion, which was exhibited as the queen's property in 1893 (*Exposicion Historico-Europea, 1892–93, Catalogo*, Sala V, No. 9). The guides who show visitors round the Treasury still (1961) perpetuate this mistake.

30 The technique employed is distinct from the usual Italian and Hungarian filigree enamel which was in vogue at the same time, in that the stamped ornaments are not attached to the ground. When the enamel flakes away, the ornaments also disappear. Examples of this technique are very rare, the Museum possesses a spoon (1392–1888) (FIG. 10) and a pair to it is in the Metropolitan Museum, New York. Until recently it has been usual to ascribe both the Toledo *nefs* to goldsmiths working for the luxurious court of the Dukes of Burgundy. Their attribution to Venice was only recently demonstrated by Dr Erich Steingräber (*Studien zür venezianischen Goldschmiedekunst* in *Mitteilungen des Kunsthistorischen Institutes in Florenz*, II, 1962, pp. 147–97). The earlier attribution was quite understandable since Venetian goldsmiths' work was heavily indebted to northern art.

31 It had a foot and not wheels (*Datos documentales para la historia del arte espanol*, III, *Inventarios reales* (*Juan II a Juana la Loca*) 1943, p. 243.

32 *Ibid*, pp. 79–80. It runs as follows: 'Una nao de cristal tiene una guarniçion de plata dorada y esmaltada y tiene debaxo quatro ruedas con sus exes y la tilla sobre que se arma y los bordes e castillos de popa e proa tode de plata dorada y esmaltada de azul y en el castil davante una sierpe eon alas esmaltadas de verde e mastilico de cristal guarneçada de una poca de plata blanca y en el copa tiene dos castillos de la misma plata dorada y tiene un pedaço de le soga de ylo de plata torçida en la proa e por la tilla unas florezicas azules debaxo de la popa azia el agua tiene a cado lado una serpezia e no tiene xarcia ni mastil ni governallo e uno de los esmaltos de las ruedas baxas esta saltada que peso veynte marcos e seys oncas e quatro ochavos.' The following is a rough translation: 'A ship of crystal having a mounting of silver, gilt and enamelled, and having underneath four wheels with their axles. And the deck on which it is fitted and the sides and the castles of the poop and of the prow are all of silver-gilt and enamelled blue. And the fo'c'sle has a serpent with wings enamelled green, and a mast of crystal mounted with a little piece of white silver and in the top are two castles of the same silver-gilt, and it has a rope of twisted silver string in the prow and along the deck are some little blue flowers. Below the poop towards the water, there are on each side a *serpezia* (?). And it has no rigging, no top-mast, no rudder, and one of the enamels of wheels underneath is missing. It weighs etc.'

33 H. Nocq, *Le Poinçon de Paris*, 1928, III, p. 79. He would also seem to have been the son of Jean le Flamenc (*d.* 1475), goldsmith, and of Thomasse his wife, who figure in the accounts of the Dukes of Burgundy (Laborde, *Les Ducs de Bourgogne*, 2nd Part, I, 1949, p. xxiii).

34 Sir Anthony Browne, created Viscount Montague in 1554, served as an ambassador on several occasions during the reigns of Mary I and Elizabeth I. The eighteenth-century viscounts who were Roman Catholics, appear to have travelled quite a lot on the Continent, and one of them might have brought the *nef* back.

35 *Gazette des Beaux-Arts*, 2nde Période, XXIII, 1881, pp. 110–11.

36 HENRICVS III GALLIARVM POLONIARVM QVE REX, HANC DEIPARAE VIRGINI NAVICVLAM, VT·RES·GALLICA·DIVTVR-NIS · IACTATA · SEDITIONVM · FLVCTIBVS · OPE · DIVINA · TANDEM · CONFERRETVR · IN TRANQVILLVM, MORE · MAJORVM·INAVGVRATVS·POSVIT·ANNO·CIƆIƆLXXII. The inscription on the other side is in slightly different lettering and reads:
DE SAINCTE VRSVLLE ET DES MIL VIERGES

C

37   Societé des Antiquaires de France, Bulletin, 1937, pp. 139–40.

38   Le Roux de Lincy, *Vie de la Reine Anne de Bretagne*, 1861, IV, p. 130.

39   E. Giraudet, *Les Artistes Tourangeaux*, 1885, p. 356. There seems to have been a tradition at Tours that a new queen should be given a *nef* when she made her first solemn entry into the city. Anne of Brittany received two *nefs* in this way. When she came as the queen of Charles VIII on 23 December 1491, she got a silver-gilt *nef* made by Jean Gallaret (E. Giraudet, *Histoire de la ville de Tours*, I, 1873, p. 268). When she came with Louis XII on 26 November 1500, she received 'une navire enrichie tout autour de pavoiz a la devise de la reine' for which Raymond Guyonnet was paid 200 écus d'or (E. Giraudet, *Les Artistes Tourangeaux*, 1885, p. 215).

40   As illustrated by Rosenberg, *Der Goldschmiede Merkzeichen*, III, No. 3687.

41   Most of the accepted works of Ludwig Krug are illustrated in an article by Otto von Falke in *Pantheon*, XI, 1933, pp. 189–94.

42   Padre Bernardo Gonzati, *Il Santuario delle Reliquie ossia il Tesoro della Basilica di S. Antonio di Padova*, Padua, 1851, pp. 42–43.

43   *Inventario degli oggetti d'arte d'Italia, Provincia di Padova, Comune di Padova*, 1936, p. 24.

44   e.g. G. Campori, *Raccolta di Cataloghi ed Inventari inediti dal sec. XV al sec. XIX, Guardaroba Estense*, 1494, Modena, 1870, pp. 10–11 and R. *Deputazione di Storia Patria per le provincie de Romagna*, III, 1909, p. 153.

45   British Museum, *Catalogue of Silver Plate, mediaeval and later bequeathed by Sir Augustus Wollaston Franks*, *1928*, pp. 24–25, where a bibliography is given.

46   Constant Lapaix, *Armorial des Villes, Bourgs et Villages de la Lorraine, du Barrois et des Trois Évêchés*, 1868, pp. 62–63, quotes an instance of the use of the motto on a jeton of 1632. The motto seems to be in some way connected with the addition of pansies to the town arms. About this Lapaix is vague but he quotes from what appears to be a fifteenth-century romance, a passage which seems to connect pansies with this town. Reference to the town archivist elicited the reply that no fresh information was available but that it was suspected that the motto was in use in the sixteenth century.

47   'Una navis arg' cum 4 rot' & 1 capite draco' deaur' ad utrumque finem e jusdem navis' *Archaeologia*, X, 1792, p. 246.

Acknowledgments

I wish to record my gratitude to the following persons who have aided me —Mr George Naish of the National Maritime Museum for advice on nautical points; Dr Günther Schiedlausky and Dr Heinrich Kohlhaussen for help on the *nef* at Nuremberg; Sr Xavier de Salas and Sr Jesús Hernández Perera for help with reference to the examples in Spain and Dr Erich Steingräber for help on the Toledo examples; Padre Antonio Sartori for discussing the example at Padua with me; Professor Urban T. Holmes, Professor Alan Boase and Miss Z. P. Zaddy for helping me to check references in early French romances and, finally, the Marquess of Exeter for his researches into the history of the Burghley Nef after it had been passed into possession of the museum.

ILLUSTRATIONS

Pl. XVIII to XX and Fig. 3. By Courtesy of Fratelli Alinari, Florence.

Pl. XII and XIII. By Courtesy of Archives Photographiques, Paris.

Fig. 15. By Courtesy of the Ashmolean Museum, Oxford.

Fig. 6. By Courtesy of the Bibliothèque Nationale, Paris.

Fig. 5. By Courtesy of Osvaldo Böhm, Venice.

Pl. XXII to XXIV and Figs. 8, 13 and 14. By Courtesy of the British Museum.

Pl. XV to XVII. By Courtesy of the Germanisches Museum, Nuremberg.

Pl. III and V. By Courtesy of Foto Mas, Barcelona.

Fig. 2. By Courtesy of Photo Club, Burgos.

Pl. I, IV and VI. By Courtesy of Rodrigues, Toledo.

CHARLES OMAN

I NEF OF ARCHBISHOP PEDRO TENORIO. Silver, parcel-gilt. Spanish (Seville); last quarter of fourteenth century. *Toledo Cathedral.* H. c. 3 ft (91·5 cm). W. c. 2 ft 3 in (64 cm)

11a FO'C'SLE OF NEF OF ARCHBISHOP TENORIO

11b FO'C'SLE OF NEF OF JUAN DE TORRELLAS

III NEF OF JUAN DE TORRELLAS. Nautilus shell mounted in silver-gilt with enamel. Spanish; first half of fifteenth century (the shell and lower part 1505). *Zaragoza Cathedral*. H. c. 2 ft (61·5 cm). W. c. 14 in (36 cm)

IV NEF OF DONA MENCIA ENRIQUEZ DE TOLEDO. Crystal and silver-gilt. Venetian; second quarter of fifteenth century. *Toledo Cathedral*. H. c. 10 in (25·5 cm). W. c. 14 in (36 cm)

V STERN OF NEF OF DONA MENCIA ENRIQUEZ DE TOLEDO

VI NEF OF JOANNA THE MAD. Crystal and silver-gilt decorated with enamel and set with gems. Venetian; third quarter of fifteenth century (the reliquary-mast, gems, and wheels, Spanish; end of sixteenth century). *Toledo Cathedral.* H. c. 2 ft 6 in (77 cm). W. c. 1 ft 6 in (46 cm)

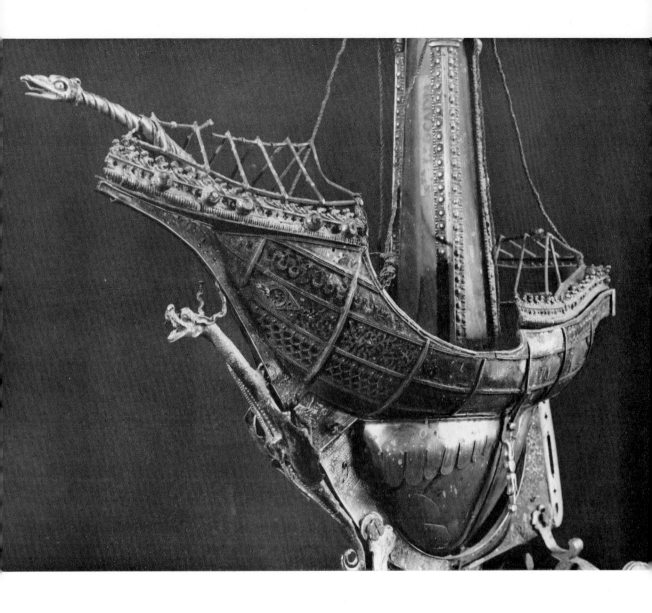

VII FO'C'SLE OF NEF OF JOANNA THE MAD

VIII THE BURGHLEY NEF. Nautilus shell mounted in silver, parcel-gilt. Made by Pierre le Flamand. Paris hall-mark for 1482–83. *Victoria & Albert Museum.* M.60–1959. H. 13⅝ in (35 cm). W. 8 in (20·5 cm)

IX THE BURGHLEY NEF (*side view*)

X THE BURGHLEY NEF (*stern*)

XI THE BURGHLEY NEF (*siren*)

XII NEF OF ANNE OF BRITTANY. Jasper, silver-gilt and gold decorated with enamel. Mark of Pierre Rousseau of Tours. About 1500 (enamelled gold figures 1505, mast 1547–59; arms and inscriptions on base 1574). *Rheims Cathedral*. H. 18⅝ in (47 cm). W. 11⅛ in (28·5 cm)

XIII NEF OF ANNE OF BRITTANY

D

XIV NEF OF ANNE OF BRITTANY (*detail of fo'c'sle*)

XV THE SCHLÜSSELFELDER NEF. Silver, parcel-gilt. Nuremberg mark; about 1503. *Lent to Germanisches National-Museum, Nuremberg.* H. 2 ft 6 in (78 cm). W. 12 in (30 cm)

XVI THE SCHLÜSSELFELDER NEF (*view from above*)

XVII THE SCHLÜSSELFELDER NEF (*stern*)

XVIII NEF. Silver, parcel-gilt. Nuremberg (?); about 1515. *Basilica di Sant' Antonio, Padua.* H. 1 ft 10⅝ in (58 cm). W. 9⅜ in (24 cm)

XIX NEF AT PADUA (*fo'c'sle*)

XX NEF AT PADUA (*poop*)

XXI NEF AT PADUA (*stern*)

XXII THE ALT DE TIEFFENTHAL NEF. Silver-gilt. French; about 1530. *British Museum*. H. 16⅓ in (42 cm). W. 8 in (20 cm)

XXIII THE ALT DE TIEFFENTHAL NEF (*fo'c'sle*)

XXIV THE ALT DE TIEFFENTHAL NEF (*stern*)